# BEYOND ENGINEERING

## How to Work on a Team

Suzanne Young and Harry T. Roman

**Professional Publications, Inc. • Belmont, CA**

## How to Locate and Report Errata for This Book

At Professional Publications, we do our best to bring you error-free books. But when errors do occur, we want to make sure you can view corrections and report any potential errors you find, so the errors cause as little confusion as possible.

A current list of known errata and other updates for this book is available on the PPI website at **www.ppi2pass.com/errata**. We update the errata page as often as necessary, so check in regularly. You will also find instructions for submitting suspected errata. We are grateful to every reader who takes the time to help us improve the quality of our books by pointing out an error.

**Beyond Engineering: How to Work on a Team**

Current printing of this edition: 1

**Printing History**

| edition number | printing number | update |
|---|---|---|
| 1 | 1 | New book. |

Copyright © 2006 by Professional Publications, Inc. All rights reserved. No part of this publication may be reproduced, stored in a retrieval system, or transmitted, in any form or by any means, electronic, mechanical, photocopying, recording, or otherwise, without the prior written permission of the publisher.

Printed in the United States of America

Professional Publications, Inc.
1250 Fifth Avenue, Belmont, CA 94002
(650) 593-9119
www.ppi2pass.com

Roman, Harry T., 1949–
 Beyond engineering : how to work on a team / Harry T. Roman and Suzanne Young.
     p. cm.
  ISBN-13: 978-1-59126-061-5
  ISBN-10: 1-59126-061-2
  1. Teams in the workplace. I. Young, Suzanne, 1948– II. Title.

HD66.R637 2006
658.4'022--dc22

2005057888

# Table of Contents

**About the Authors** . . . . . . . . . . . . . . . . . . . . . . . . . . . . . . . . . . . . . . . . . v
**Acknowledgments** . . . . . . . . . . . . . . . . . . . . . . . . . . . . . . . . . . . . . . . vii
**Introduction** . . . . . . . . . . . . . . . . . . . . . . . . . . . . . . . . . . . . . . . . . . . . ix
    1    If It Were Simple, You Wouldn't Need a Team. . . . . . . . . . . . . . . . . 1
    2    Collaborative Styles. . . . . . . . . . . . . . . . . . . . . . . . . . . . . . . . . . 9
    3    Project Basics. . . . . . . . . . . . . . . . . . . . . . . . . . . . . . . . . . . . . 15
    4    Becoming a Team . . . . . . . . . . . . . . . . . . . . . . . . . . . . . . . . . . 23
    5    Creating Ownership . . . . . . . . . . . . . . . . . . . . . . . . . . . . . . . . 31
    6    The Value of Conflict. . . . . . . . . . . . . . . . . . . . . . . . . . . . . . . . 37
    7    Communications. . . . . . . . . . . . . . . . . . . . . . . . . . . . . . . . . . . 45
    8    Cultivating Creativity . . . . . . . . . . . . . . . . . . . . . . . . . . . . . . . . 55
    9    Beyond Technical Knowledge . . . . . . . . . . . . . . . . . . . . . . . . . 59
   10    Assembling Resources . . . . . . . . . . . . . . . . . . . . . . . . . . . . . . 65
   11    Some Special Teams . . . . . . . . . . . . . . . . . . . . . . . . . . . . . . . . 77
**Additional Reading** . . . . . . . . . . . . . . . . . . . . . . . . . . . . . . . . . . . . . 89
**Index** . . . . . . . . . . . . . . . . . . . . . . . . . . . . . . . . . . . . . . . . . . . . . . . 91

# About the Authors

Suzanne Young is a writer, editor, and communications consultant. She writes for Fortune 500 companies and for trade and consumer magazines. Her work has appeared in *San Francisco Chronicle Magazine*, *Forward Magazine*, and others.

A former corporate communications executive, Ms. Young consults with senior executives on communications strategy and corporate culture. Her book-length works for corporations include guides to conducting effective meetings, effective communications for managers, and making investment decisions in 401k plans. She is co-editor of and contributor to *Works of Heart: Building Village through the Arts*, from New Village Press. She was the developmental editor for *Designing Brand Identity* by Alina R. Wheeler.

She holds a master of fine arts degree in creative nonfiction from Goucher College and a bachelor of arts in journalism from Temple University. She lives in San Francisco with her husband Allan and has a love/hate relationship with sailing the challenging waters of the San Francisco Bay.

If you have suggestions, ideas, or comments about this book, or if it helped you in your job, Suzanne Young would enjoy hearing from you by email through PPIs web form, www.ppi2pass.com/errata.

Harry T. Roman is a senior technology consultant for PSE&G Company. He has published over 400 technical papers, articles, and monographs, and has authored or co-authored several books. He holds nine U.S. patents, and chairs the New Jersey Inventors Hall of Fame. During his 35-year engineering career, Mr. Roman has developed new technology for every phase of a modern utility system, from nuclear power plants to wooden pole lines. An expert in the use of robotic devices in utility applications, he is generally acknowledged as the "father" of the technology in the United States.

Since 1985, Mr. Roman has taught graduate management engineering courses at the New Jersey Institute of Technology, specializing in R&D project management and new product development. He has also taught courses in leadership, management, communications, coaching and counseling, and delegation and motivation.

Throughout his career, he has been active with local schools, bringing science, technology, and invention to life in the classroom. Mr. Roman writes regularly for national educational magazines including *Highlights for Children, Techdirections, The Technology Teacher, Teaching K-8,* and *TIES*.

# Acknowledgments

To the engineers, project managers, and consultants who so generously shared their insights and practical experiences, I extend my gratitude. Special thanks to Susan Wheelan for sharing her vast experience in working with teams within the engineering community. Many thanks to Connie Kirby whose insights were invaluable and whose instinctive networking skills connected me with such qualified and interesting people. To Curt Francis, our conversations were such a pleasure. To Bill Schneider, thanks for your inspiring work. To Frederic Laurentine, John Headland, Curt Edwards, Donald Apy, and Steve Winshel, thank you for sharing your time-tested experiences. Thanks also to Steven M. Horner, principal of Horner & Associates, LLC, and Elliott Ross, Ed.D., for your insights. Thank you to the editors of Knowledge@Wharton, the on-line research and business analysis journal of the Wharton School of the University of Pennsylvania, for permission to quote David Sirota. Grateful acknowledgment is made to Bruce Tuckman for permission to quote from B.W. Tuckman, "Developmental sequence in small groups," *Psychological Bulletin* 63 (1965): 384-399. And, finally, thank you to Harry T. Roman, author of *Building Internal Team-Partnerships*, from which this book evolved.

—Suzanne Young

# Introduction

## WHY ON EARTH WOULD YOU WANT TO WORK ON A TEAM?

Companies are fond of saying that people are their greatest asset.

But there's a second part left unsaid. That statement is true only if their people can work together.

Perhaps you've made it this far in your career always working alone, and you're finding that that's changing. If the boundaries of your comfort zone go only as far as your own computer, then this book is for you.

In most organizations, it's very likely you'll need to collaborate in many ways. You might work with clients, with other engineers, with people in marketing or sales, with reps from the manufacturing side of things, with the quality assurance people. A person who can work with ease on a team has a better chance of a successful and rewarding career.

Perhaps a customer has engaged your firm to tackle a problem. Or maybe the client with the problem is another department in your own company. Either way, if you insist on thinking of yourself as the Lone Ranger, you'll be hard pressed to create a complete solution for anyone. Working on a team not only spreads the responsibility, it increases the store of knowledge available for a comprehensive solution.

It also shares the stress. On a team, you have people to brainstorm with when you're stuck, to commiserate with when solutions come slowly—and to celebrate success with when everything pays off.

This book takes a look at the process by which teams become effective. It's not mysterious. There are basic rules of the road. Sure, there are obstacles that every team faces. These can be overcome with some insight and practice. Learn how to work on a team and you become a person readily identified as someone who can get things done.

## TEN REASONS TO WORK ON A TEAM

1. You get to work with other really smart people.
2. Other team members are smart in areas you're not.
3. You have people to test your ideas on.
4. Ideas increase exponentially in groups.
5. Teams are faster and more productive than individuals.
6. There's support during tough times.
7. A team has more nerve to try new things.
8. A team has more persuasive impact in selling the idea than an individual has.
9. The solution ends up being richer and more comprehensive.
10. You're not alone.

# 1

# If It Were Simple, You Wouldn't Need a Team

*Companies face challenges that no one person can possibly solve.*

Working alone, Henry Ford built a gas engine on his kitchen table. Bill Gates holed up in his dorm room while he and Paul Allen developed the software that launched the PC revolution. Dave Packard and Bill Hewlett developed their first product in a garage.

These corporate legends keep alive the notion that you can do it alone—create the new thing that changes the culture. But in reality, the lone inventor tinkering away in the basement would get further in less time if he or she could draw on the expertise of people from a variety of disciplines and with a wide range of skills.

To survive in business, you must be able to convert knowledge into continual improvement and rapid innovation. The virtual explosion in the quantity and accessibility of new information means there is more to know than any

It could be a product development team, a quality improvement team, even a crisis team. A team brings people of diverse skills and capabilities together to accomplish a goal. The size of the team varies according to the scope of the project. On projects with a wide scope, the team might include a series of sub-teams, each working on a different aspect of the total project.

One factor that distinguishes successful projects is the way people from different disciplines interact.

*In effective project teams, members know how to listen to each other, how to fight, how to resolve issues, all for the expressed purpose of building the best solution.*

That's not to imply that everything is precise and perfect. It's not. If it's human, it's messy. And in the often messy process of working on a project team, people learn from each other.

A single successful project team might be a happy accident. A pattern of successful project teams, though, usually indicates someone has provided the means for success. Here are a few of them.

Successful teams

- know what the corporate priorities are
- listen to their customers and internal client departments
- are "we" oriented
- understand the strategic value of technology
- know how to innovate and bring new products and services into being

Companies that know how to form effective teams encourage partnerships among employees from different departments, and sometimes also with customers, outside agencies, and regulators. These companies recognize that it takes skill to work well as a team, so they provide training. They look for internal barriers that can prevent success, and they remove them.

## IF IT WERE SIMPLE, YOU WOULDN'T NEED A TEAM

Whether the services or products that a team is developing are meant for use by an internal department or an external marketplace, the competitive stakes are high. And unforgiving. Do you really know what Europe will want from your company's products next year? How about Asia? Do you know what the competition has on the horizon? What about the best marketing strategy?

Sure, you could research it all, but do you have time? The intelligence you need can be obtained faster and more accurately by including the right people on your team. The most efficient way for a company to tackle these complex issues is to assemble a team that combines technical know-how, competitive intelligence, and customer insight with legal and technical savvy.

It used to be that about one new product in 50 became a commercial success. Today, depending on the industry, the mortality rate is even greater. New product development in particular has a high casualty rate. About three-quarters of these failures can be traced to a lack of communication and teamwork between major departments. Collaboration could have saved the new product, not to mention the lost investment of time and people.

## BUT I NEVER PLAYED SOCCER

Learning to work on a team might come easily if you've played a sport like basketball or soccer. But even if you haven't, don't worry. Working on a team is a discipline, and it can be learned. There's no magic formula, and you won't be able to measure it precisely. But you *will* recognize a well-functioning team when you see it—and so will your internal and external customers.

Without much conscious thought, you have almost certainly already learned some things about partnerships and collaborations. You've probably participated in some collaborative experiences of one form or another, even though you probably don't think of them as "team" experiences. The following are just a few of the collaborations many of us function in at times.

- family
- friendships
- schools and classes

- romantic relationships
- marriage
- religious groups
- professional organizations
- sports teams
- societies
- civic and fraternal groups
- neighborhoods and communities

Most people join clubs and organizations because they're meaningful. They're fun. They're rewarding. You get a good feeling from participating. It's possible to bring the same vibrancy and satisfaction you get from these relationships to your job.

But work isn't always about fun. And if you're honest, your motivation at work might not be about being a good corporate citizen. Sure, the company hopes you will be one. But it's more about not wasting your time—making the most effective use of the skills you bring to the table, and delivering a solution that works.

### Thomas Edison: An Early Team Builder

Which of Edison's inventions was the most important? You might point to the phonograph, the electric light, or motion pictures. But while each changed the world and the way we experience it, Edison's most dramatic invention was the industrial laboratory.

Edison invented the process of what we might call collaborative invention. He pioneered the use of teams and partnerships to get work problems solved quickly and profitably. Today, he and his coworkers would be considered high-performance teams.

In their New Jersey laboratories, they devoted themselves to solving problems with deep enthusiasm, often staying late to hammer out a new invention. They regularly ate meals together, a pleasant and effective way to talk out issues.

The process of collaborating can be as important as the product or service being created. Learn the process and you can participate in the power of intelligent and creative minds to exceed expectations.

## FEELING CONNECTED

Within very large companies, it's easy to feel isolated or unimportant. That's another benefit of working on a project team. In medium to large companies, teams can inject some of the closeness and intimacy that characterize small, agile companies. It may be the only place where you feel "we're all in this together."

A team can create a niche within an otherwise impersonal culture through its members' collaborative efforts and passion around the work. When a project team really gets going, it exudes an *esprit de corps*. You can sense it. When a team is working well, relying on and inspiring each other to create the best solution, you can feel the genuine excitement and satisfaction around the work. The team owns the process of solving the problem, ownership translates into smart solutions, and the company becomes filled with problem solvers instead of people waiting to be told what to do. You can't help but soak up the energy and get involved yourself.

## GET THERE FASTER

It all adds up to getting people to do something together in support of a common goal. After all, what's the point of your advanced knowledge if you can't create real-world solutions?

Working collaboratively is efficient. Communication flows well. People on the team share insights and knowledge. Close cooperation between technical specialists and customers or internal client departments leads more quickly to high quality products and services.

To create successful teams and successful projects, there are some basic rules of the road. They'll help your team move the group through the developmental stages faster and with less disruption. That's what this book is designed to do.

# 2

# Collaborative Styles

*Working on a team involves a formal commitment of human, technical, and financial resources.*

Imagine yourself as a project engineer within a medium-sized company. Several departments need your expertise to solve a problem.

You can work with people who need your expertise in several ways.

- as a *consultant*
- as a *member of a team*
- as an *intrapreneur*

As a *consultant*, you might get an occasional request for your services. A department head might ask you for advice or some minimal research.

Or you could participate in a full-fledged *project team* to tackle a problem and build a solution.

At a more senior level, you might act as an *internal entrepreneur*, spotting a potential fit between a technology and a need, and taking the initiative to get a project going.

It wouldn't be unusual for a busy professional to fulfill multiple roles at the same time. Don't underestimate the consulting role, though. You might find it such an integral part of your daily work that you don't even recognize how important this is.

## THE CONSULTANT

In your consulting role, think of yourself as a catalyst in a chemical reaction.

Your role might be informal and relatively brief, but your input changes the nature of the situation. Your professional contacts and information, for example, might be just the key piece of information to push a project along. Your work could be as simple as a few telephone calls or moving some key research results or reports to others who are at work on a project. A client department might request your help. Or you might see that you have something to contribute and take the initiative.

The work also may be more involved—researching the literature or making some sample calculations, for example. Although it may appear to be a low-profile role, it lubricates the operational gears.

In fact, most of the time a good project engineer plays this role, by interacting with company contacts, answering telephone calls or inquiries, and moving information around to interested individuals. Often it's your responsibility to make the contacts and establish the channels of communication within the company.

In your role as a consultant, you'll respond to direct queries and give helpful but unsolicited information. Diplomacy is an important skill when providing unsolicited information, as your good intentions should not be misinterpreted as interfering.

Here are some typical activities in a consulting role.

- answering telephone requests and providing general follow-up to requests for information
- circulating reports and information relevant to client department projects and concerns
- performing calculations or making recommendations in response to client needs
- recommending vendors or other contact sources that can help a client department solve a problem
- acting as an interface to outside agencies to obtain needed information
- demonstrating a new piece of technology for the client's benefit

## THE TEAM MEMBER

You might be tapped to serve on a project team. Let's say you are assigned to a formal project with people from other departments. Your mission may be to improve the performance of an existing process, technology, or outcome. The following chapters explore your role on a team in more depth.

Working on a team is different from the consulting role in several important respects. You are

- officially assigned to the project
- responsible for helping to define the problem and assembling the resources
- responsible for contributing ideas to the potential solution
- a contributor to project communications
- aware of and ready to seek outside funding if possible to support the work

Working on a team is deeper and more participatory than the consultant role. It involves a formal commitment of human, technical and financial resources to the project effort, and requires specific management approval.

## THE INTRAPRENEUR

The role of the internal entrepreneur is the one in which you act as a self-starting advocate or champion for solutions that can be of value to the company. In this role, you could be completely responsible for conceptualizing and the internal marketing of new products or services to other departments. It is a self-initiated process, likely to be assumed only by senior people. Its success relies on a mature network of interdepartmental contacts.

The intrapreneur might be attempting to foster large-scale innovation. It is a role that carries risk. Success hinges on interpersonal and marketing skills. In its most highly developed state, it may take the form of a skunkworks (see below).

Even if you're not an intrapreneur yourself, you might find yourself supporting the work of one. You'll probably see a different method of interaction with client departments. The intrapreneur may begin with a company-wide task force to solicit opinions from a wide variety of potential client departments. It's especially useful in revealing which departments are potential target markets for the innovation. Once these potential markets are identified, the intrapreneur can design specific project efforts with formalized project teams. The initial task force phase can generally extend from six months to a year, or possibly longer, depending on the scope and depth of the mission.

---

**Skunkworks: The Ultimate Team**

You won't see this often, but it's certainly worth a mention. A skunkworks is a sort of super team. The team members not only work cooperatively on the project, they temporarily dedicate their careers to it, doing nothing else.

A skunkworks often operates under the radar, off-site and off-budget. A company resorts to a skunkworks when it's trying to create something radically new, or when faced with unusual or threatening financial conditions. A skunkworks is often moved to an off-site location so its members can work away from the distractions of ongoing responsibilities, focusing only on the task at hand.

The business meaning of the word originated in 1943. A team at aircraft manufacturer Lockheed Martin took on an assignment in strict secrecy to develop a new jet fighter to aid the allied forces during World War II. Their mission: build an airframe around the powerful British Goblin jet engine. To meet the deadline the team moved off-site and worked much like an entrepreneurial start-up.

They delivered the XP-80 in 143 days, seven days ahead of schedule. They called themselves Skunk Works, after the Skonk Works in the popular comic strip of the day *Li'l Abner*, where two characters brewed illicit moonshine that reeked of skunks and old shoes, among other things. Lockheed Martin's development team dubbed themselves Skunk Works because their temporary location was next to a smelly factory. Skunk Works is now a registered trademark of Lockheed Martin.

An excellent description of how a skunkworks operates on a day-to-day basis can be found in *The Soul of a New Machine*, by Tracy Kidder. A classic in the literature of innovation, the book follows Data General Corporation's efforts to develop a new computer. It traces the emotional and intellectual investment that the team put into the project. Most teams never get elevated to this level, but when one does, it will be quite an experience.

# 3

# Project Basics

*Projects are never single-discipline projects,
even when you think they are.*

—Curt Francis

Even though you've just been assigned to a new project team, you can already expect the project to follow a predictable evolution. Each project will be different, but there are six typical steps in a project's lifecycle, as shown in the following illustration.

### Step 1
### Define the Problem

Before you can begin to design a solution, your first task is to understand the problem. It sounds obvious, but it's really not. This step may be the most important part of the entire project lifecycle.

It's the project team's job to make an accurate diagnosis rather than accept the client's assessment of the problem at face value. The client may be partly right, but the team may uncover other underlying issues that will lead to a better, more complete solution.

### The Project Life Cycle

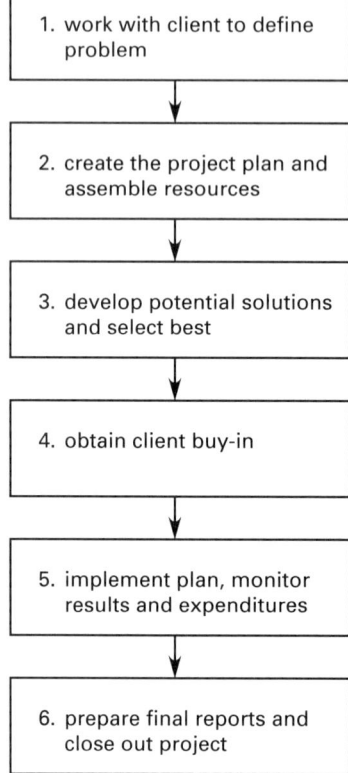

Allow enough time in this stage of the project to investigate the problem thoroughly. Examine the immediate technical problem, and then look beyond it for larger strategic issues. To get below the surface requires you to understand the business issues that are important to your client.

Curt Francis, an experienced project manager, says when a team assumes that it knows everything it needs to know, look out. "Projects are never single-discipline projects, even when you think they are. There are always technology issues. There may be finance issues, or legal issues."

# 3 PROJECT BASICS

Understanding the issue in depth may change the composition of your project team. If you integrate sales, marketing, product development, and service functions into the team, rather than keeping a purely technical focus, your solution will be richer. You can bundle products, service, and delivery options to meet specific customer needs.

## Understand the Business Problem, Not Just the Technical Problem

Steve Winshel has been a senior executive for information technology with a number of companies, ranging from start-ups with a handful of employees to mid-size companies with up to 15,000 employees. He has led or mentored project teams for nearly two decades. Over the course of his career as an executive and a consultant, Winshel has brought many developers and engineers into their first project team experiences, as well as their first management experiences in the role of team leader on small projects.

"Rarely is a project clear-cut," Winshel says. "Even if there is an apparent solution to the problem we're trying to solve, it usually changes as we dig into the solution. It's not as easy as it might appear. Never is it like having a 27-piece Lego set that I can put it in front of the team and say, 'Here's the problem; the task for the five of you is to put it together.'"

Winshel observes that it is the natural inclination of engineers to focus single-mindedly on a technical solution and single-mindedly pursue it. Then, "when they throw their solution over the wall to the customer, and it's rejected, they're surprised."

He recommends bringing engineering team members into customer meetings as early as possible, rather than waiting for a hand-off of specific tasks, to help them understand the business problem in a larger way.

"In the case of a manufacturing system for a medical device company, there was a problem with users on the manufacturing line—too much time was being spent on a particular step in the manufacturing process. While the obvious solution was to develop new software to speed that phase, there were underlying issues that later redirected the way solutions were implemented. Until you start getting into it, you don't really know."

## What Does the Problem *Mean*?

During her tenure as a professor at a university, Susan Wheelan was asked to chair a newly formed multidisciplinary teaching academy. The mission of the academy was "to improve the quality of teaching and learning" within the university.

"That's huge. What does that mean? How would we do it? Who else would work on it? How would it be structured? How would we benchmark it? A lot of projects are like that," Wheelan says. "A client might say, 'Build us a better communications array.' Well, what does that mean?"

That's what the team has to find out before it can start building solutions. It's the team's job to investigate the problem from every angle. Before you even think about a solution, do you know what the client expects? It's a good idea to agree on a definition of what a successful outcome is at the front end. Define the metrics you'll use to assess its effectiveness.

Winshel recommends including engineers from the project team in design-level meetings with the client business unit. "If you have the right engineering person in the room at this stage, they can tell the client if they're heading in an impossible direction. If the business unit knew that early on, it would fundamentally change the odds for success before the project even starts."

The takeaway: The project may seem clearly defined, but at the outset *you don't know what you don't know*. The obvious and immediate technical solution may turn out to be only a bandage instead of a long-term solution. Spend as much time as you can with the customer to understand the larger business problem. Bring some highly experienced people from different disciplines with you.

- Focus the problem so an organized plan of action or work statement can be developed from strategic, technical, and cost standpoints. This is where you begin to learn what you don't know.
- Present your findings in terms of the business impact on efficiency, customer satisfaction, and profitability.
- Obtain commitments for resources, including people, equipment, and funding.

# 3 PROJECT BASICS

## *Step 2*
## Create the Project Plan and Assemble Resources

Review the formal project plan for the implementation of the project. This plan should include the following.

- the problem or need, and why it should be solved
- the plan of action, expressed as distinct project phases
- the resources required
- the expected benefits
- benchmarks and metrics to measure the success of solution
- other departments and/or outside consultants to be involved
- the implementation schedule and personnel required
- the project budget and departmental allocations
- a schedule of reports and managerial checkpoints
- deliverable products, services, and/or output

Once this project plan is refined and accepted by the team members and the management of all departments involved, it becomes the blueprint for the project. Make sure you have a copy. It is the reference for briefing management on the project's progress and expenditures. It will also contain the necessary information for developing annual budgetary and project approval requests.

The project plan can have another important use: as a basis for soliciting outside funding support from state, federal, or industry agencies in those circumstances when a company seeks outside partners. A well-written plan can demonstrate to a funding authority that a company thoroughly understands an industry problem and is committed to a solution.

Any number of resources exists to support the project. They could be internal or external. They might be technological or human. A resource might be as simple as a corporate library search or a literature review. Or you might find yourself assigned to an industry task force or other working group to gain the necessary information and bring it back to the team. See Ch. 10 for a more detailed look at potential resources. Your project manager should identify, orchestrate, and blend the flow of those resources.

## Step 3
### Develop Potential Solutions

During this phase of the process, information flows freely among team members. Work is at a peak. Activities might include a paper study or assessment, or the development and/or field testing of prototypical equipment.

This phase might involve a wide spectrum of contacts with an external community. Team members might also enrich the outside community with company-developed information in the form of project results and technical papers. From one or more technical solutions, your team must ultimately select a candidate solution.

Your choice will be influenced by two factors: how well the solution meets the project's philosophy and original justification, and how cost-effective it is overall. Possible synergies and benefits to other potential users could also influence the decision.

## Step 4
### Sell the Solution

Keeping your client up to speed with your team's progress allows the client to evolve along with the team as its thinking progresses. Few things are more demotivating to a project team than to have its solution rejected as too impractical or expensive.

Staying in touch with the client also precludes being surprised with new information that renders your solution invalid. Keeping clients involved gives them a vested interest in the project, which is a real asset at this vital stage.

But there's no guarantee that your team's work will be accepted. Sometimes a solution can be hampered not for technical reasons but for reasons that have to do with human nature and tradition. These could include

- doubts regarding a new and untested technology
- changes to accepted operating procedures
- conflict with labor relations rules and practices
- first use of a technology with no maintenance history

Don't be surprised if management, biased by previous experience, views your solution with some skepticism. Frequent project reviews with management will help avoid serious problems at this stage. While it may not be your job to schedule these reviews, you can point out potential opportunities for misunderstandings so the team can address them.

## *Step 5*
### Implementation

Once the team begins actual implementation, it's natural to put your head down, focus only on the work, and charge ahead. It's a good idea to keep your client and other interested groups up to date with your progress, as well as with any unexpected pitfalls you encounter. Rarely is an implementation as smooth as it appears to be in the design phase. Maintaining good communication will help to speed your resolution of these problems and help to keep you on schedule.

## *Step 6*
### Close Out

When the project is completed, the reports and documentation the team prepares serves as a record of its work. It may also form the springboard for a future project team, should there be an opportunity to take the work to another level of development.

# 4

# Becoming a Team

*Only one in four American workers has worked on a well-functioning team. Most people think they hate teams because they haven't had good models.*

—Susan Wheelan

Anyone who has led or been a member of a project team will agree that a well-functioning team is a pleasure to participate in. How do you know you're on a good one?

According to Susan Wheelan, who studies team performance, the signs are unmistakable.

- It's exciting.
- You can't wait to go to the meetings.
- You feel like a grown-up.
- Your input is valued.

- You value the input of your team members.
- The idea gets better because of the dialogue.
- You can disagree without being rejected.

But most of us, at one time or another, have served on a team that didn't function well. The symptoms are all too painfully familiar.

- You don't know why you're there in the first place.
- People don't talk in meetings.
- Meetings are long and boring, and accomplish nothing.
- Input is dismissed or ignored.
- The idea is off base and going nowhere.
- Team members snipe at each other.
- There's little support for the team leader.
- The team leader just likes to hear himself talk.

Most teams are a unique blend of people with varying skills, experience, and personalities.

And just as in the old saying that opposites attract but they have difficulty living together, teams are no different. People who are different make a better team in the long run in terms of the result they produce, but only if they learn to work together.

Just putting a group of people together doesn't make a team. But what does?

*Teams come together around the work, not around team building.*

As with any group of people working together for the first time, it will take a while for the team to work smoothly. But every team, whether aware of it or not, follows the same process of development. This should be reassuring!

# THE TUCKMAN MODEL

The four stages of group or team development were first articulated in 1965 by Bruce Tuckman. He identified these stages as

1. forming
2. storming
3. norming
4. performing

Whether you're a team member or the project team leader, you'll be ahead of the game if you understand which phase your team is in at any given time. Then you'll be able to anticipate the normal bumps along the way.

## Stage One
### Forming

This is the introductory stage when team members meet each other and begin to learn about the purpose of the team.

The team leader introduces the team's mission—the problem to be solved. Members learn about each other's skills and anticipated contributions. The project lead acts as a buffer between the team and the rest of the organization. This buys the group enough time to figure out how to get going.

In this stage, people wear their party manners. They generally go with the flow. They hang back to see how things work, checking out who's who.

### Suggestions for Stage One

- Get to know the people you are working with as best as you can. What are their areas of expertise? What other assets do they bring to the team?
- Suggest having a team meeting over lunch.
- If the project launch involves an off-site meeting, expect some relaxation time when people can socialize or hang out. People who can laugh together can usually come together faster as a team.

**Some thoughts that might run through your mind in Stage One**

- Why am I here?
- Where do I sit?

## Stage Two
### Storming

Team members begin to feel confident enough to examine and challenge the project assumptions or the way the team is working. Some people jockey for position in this phase. Conflicts and disagreements develop. Patterns for how conflict gets resolved are established now.

Making decisions during this stage is not efficient because the team is only beginning to learn how to work together. Stage Two is when team members begin to assert themselves. The group may settle into small cliques.

Different personalities annoy or grate on each other. The party manners start to come off.

The team leader needs to direct the group. An experienced team leader will welcome the challenges that are raised without becoming defensive. Even though the group may have already made some basic decisions, give the team plenty of opportunity to revisit these decisions and refine them. That accomplishes two valuable things: the team starts taking ownership of the project, and the idea continues to get better.

**How to recognize Stage Two**

- Members start challenging the team leader. *Why do we have to do this?*
- Members challenge the operating rules the team has agreed to. *Everybody has to be on time to meetings? Not true. Where's Robert? He's always late.*
- Deadlocks are common.

**Suggestions for Stage Two**

- Listen.
- Speak up.
- If the goal's not clear, say so.

# 4 BECOMING A TEAM

- Make sure you know what you're supposed to do.
- If you're not the right person to do your assigned aspect of the project, say so.

## Stage Three
### Norming

The team leader helps members buy in to the mission of the team. Now the group begins to feel like a unit. Individuals are clear about their own roles and responsibilities, as well as those of their teammates.

Everyone understands how the team will make decisions. Because of this, the team begins to make decisions faster. The team is becoming proficient at communicating with its clients and the rest of the organization. The process of functioning as a team begins to feel easier and more streamlined.

Team members begin to trust each other. Individuals begin to share leadership. The team understands its scope of authority. The team organizes communications with the rest of the company. The team leader's role becomes less authoritative and more facilitative.

Members begin to understand that their job is the same as the team leader, which is to create a high-performance collaborative team together.

### Suggestions for Stage Three

- Listen.
- Support the team with suggestions and ideas.
- Pitch in where needed.
- Raise issues that may become roadblocks.
- Acknowledge the good work of your fellow team members.

## Stage Four
### Performing

The work proceeds intently. The team is comfortable with open dialogue around the product or solution. Communications flow freely, not just from management down, but from the team up to management, and laterally to clients and other groups interested in the work. Members introduce differing points of view without fear of retaliation, and conflicts are resolved quickly, without rancor. Team members share a philosophical and spiritual commitment to the project and to each other. Members take responsibility for group performance. People enjoy working together.

At this stage, if the unexpected happens—and it will—members of a well-functioning team step up and assume responsibility for meeting off-plan challenges. Whether it's a change in schedule or in a design spec, the team owns the project. Members agree on how to handle the problem without expecting the project lead to micromanage it. The project lead now functions more as a member than as the leader.

Personalities who may have clashed in an earlier stage now accept each other as they focus on the work. If the person who drove you crazy at the first meeting now makes you shake your head and smile to yourself, congratulations! You've moved from thinking, "he's a jerk" to "well, he's still a jerk, but he's *our* jerk." That's when you know you're a team.

**Suggestions for Stage Four**

- Challenge the work.
- Bring intelligence back to the team to make the work better.
- Be flexible and change as needed.
- Anticipate team needs.

## KNOWING WHICH STAGE YOU'RE IN

The team that understands these four stages will be better prepared when, after a couple of months, the first fight breaks out. It's reassuring to know that if, for example, everyone is arguing, it just means you're in Stage Two! Then team members can engage in and resolve the conflict, rather than back away from it. As Wheelan says, "They'll start to really vocalize disagreement and think, 'Oh good, we're moving into the conflict stage!' as opposed to thinking, 'These people are really maniacs!'"

But if you're still in Stage Two months and months later, someone needs to call for help.

## What you can do

- Read a book on group development.
- Take a course on working in teams.
- Speak up.
- Stay focused on the work, not on other people.
- Listen!

## HIGH PERFORMANCE IS MORE THAN LUCK

A high-performing team rarely happens by accident—it takes work. A team leader who can help the group through the developmental phases is indispensable. With skill and insight, a team leader can enable team members to build a shared commitment to the task at hand and to each other.

The stages that lead to becoming a well-functioning team are documented and predictable. What can't be predicted is the way any one team will evolve and how long each stage will take. Some groups evolve into high-performing teams but never really know how they got that way. Others remain stuck in a phase and never get beyond it.

Even high-performing teams can regress to an earlier stage. For instance, if one team member is replaced with a new member, the team instantly reverts back to Stage One, though it will progress through the stages faster than it did the first time. So it takes constant checking and adjusting to keep a team focused on performance and moving forward.

# 5

# Creating Ownership

*Camaraderie, although it is not mentioned much, is key—not only in the sense of having a friend, but working well together as a team. That is a tremendous source of satisfaction for people.*
—David Sirota

The dynamic energy that radiates from a sense of ownership is the result of actions that tell the team its work is important. Team members develop a sense of empowerment when they get real affirmation, not just lip service. That affirmation can come from fellow team members, from the project manager, or from management at higher levels. Ideally, it comes from all three.

Your team might be enthusiastic on the first day. But real ownership begins to take hold as the team develops into a group that performs. This usually begins in Stage Three (norming) and really develops in Stage Four (performing).

Empowerment comes when teams

- see the relevance of their work within the larger corporate picture
- have the autonomy to make decisions about their work

- are proud of the quality and high standard of their work
- respect their fellow team members for their talents and contributions
- see that management both respects and values their work

## THE EMPOWERMENT PYRAMID

A sense of ownership happens when specific elements are present. Without them, the team won't come together.

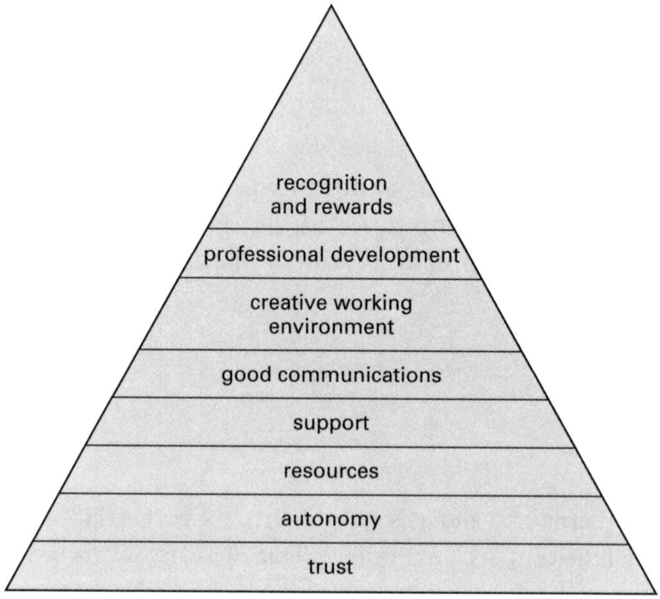
recognition
and rewards
professional development
creative working
environment
good communications
support
resources
autonomy
trust

### Trust

The foundation of the pyramid, the most important building block, is trust. Without it, teams cannot and will not form a passionate commitment to the project.

To be motivated to take ownership of their work, members must be able to trust the team leader and each other. Many elements go into creating trust, but the most critical—and perhaps the most surprising—is knowing how to

# 5 CREATING OWNERSHIP

express and resolve conflicting points of view. Chapter 6 covers this important aspect of working as a team.

## Autonomy

Hand in hand with trust goes delegated authority. Effective team leaders delegate decision making to the people who know their jobs better than their managers. It's an act that extends power to the team.

Few things will demotivate a team more than if its members find out they have less authority than they thought. When team decisions are countermanded by a higher authority, motivation can be measured in negative numbers. Every team needs to be clear about its scope of authority.

- What can you make decisions about autonomously?
- Which decisions must be reviewed and approved by other groups?

Teams must be able to make decisions that are relevant to the work. If they are handed all the decisions, their logical response might be, "Why don't you just do it yourself?" A team without a voice is just a group of people.

Yet autonomy has its limits. The team must stay connected with the rest of the organization.

If it's not clear how far the team's authority extends, get it on the table immediately. Push for clarification. Be specific. Establishing clarity early will get the team performing faster.

## Resources

These fall into three general areas: equipment, people, and money. Teams need access to adequate resources to get the job done. Check out Ch. 10 for a full discussion on where to look for additional resources when you've hit the wall.

## Support

Support comes from management, from the team leader, and from fellow team members. In fact, about 15 percent of all statements made in teams that are working well are supportive of other team members. You won't be able to force upper management to be supportive, but you can support your colleagues. Acknowledge their good work. Let them share the limelight. Your enthusiasm and spirit can be contagious.

## Good Communications

The team should be able to communicate its findings, concerns, and feelings upward on a regular basis. If stifled, the team will quickly lose interest. It's a short path from there to believing that your work is neither important nor appreciated. You can tell when a team is disempowered. They'll wait for the project leader to tell them what to do and then dutifully fulfill the assignment without inspiration or pride in the work. There's more about communications in Ch. 7.

## Creative Working Environment

Setting and environment definitely can influence your ability to think creativity. Simply knowing that you have the freedom and flexibility to try something new or to explore different areas enables you to think unconventionally. See Ch. 8 for some ideas about thinking creatively.

## Professional Development

In the course of working with other bright minds, you will encounter new ideas, gain new insights, and, ideally, learn from other team members. Expect to gain a broader perspective on your own job and a new appreciation for your ability to contribute to the company's performance. If you've worked on a good team, it will be an experience that has given you and each member an opportunity to grow professionally. At the close of the assignment, you should walk away with a broader and deeper knowledge than when you began.

# 5 CREATING OWNERSHIP

## Recognition and Rewards

Let's face it: Money is important. In an ideal world, we're passionate about the work. *And* we really like getting paid for it. Team members are often compensated with bonuses or special payments for participating in projects that go above and beyond their normal scope of work.

Teams need recognition from upper management about the value of their work in the company's overall strategy. Both acknowledgment and monetary rewards are appropriate for teams.

### Different Departments, Different Rewards

A project team usually includes individuals from different departments. But what if these different departments reward people differently for participating on the team?

Fredric Laurentine, as a project manager, solved this problem after much thought.

"The team I worked with had people from operations, manufacturing, and marketing. Each had ongoing jobs. And each of those departments had very different notions of what appropriate rewards were for serving on a special team. So it was possible for inequity to exist, which certainly set up conflicts among the team. If one person got $500 for being on the team and another got $5,000 for the same relative contribution, it created real conflict.

"Often rewards were given for meeting the ship date. So we'd end up with the best possible product by the ship date, instead of focusing on the best product. So one thing I did was to change the requirements for receiving a bonus. We built a quality factor into the equation. Did the product perform well after several months? It was more than just getting the product out the door.

"I also looked at the size of the contribution of each member. Some people were involved every day. Others with special expertise came in for shorter intervals. We wanted to reward great contributions over an extended time period, rather than spectacular diving catches."

Good conflict focuses on the work. Conflict that focuses on individuals is the kind that poisons teams. Learning how to disagree and resolve the disagreement is an important skill for every team to master. Without it, it's impossible to achieve the level of a well-performing team.

Remember the Empowerment Pyramid from Ch. 5? The foundation of that pyramid is trust. By mastering conflict, team members begin to trust each other. Only by realizing that you can disagree with each other and not get killed will you develop trust. Trust is the single most important quality in a team that works well together.

## TWO RULES ABOUT CONFLICT

### Rule 1
### Task Conflict is Good

Task conflict focuses on the work, not the person.

> *This wiring diagram is inefficient. It would work much better if we connected A to B instead of C.*
>
> *This approach is flawed. It works for IT, but it doesn't work for manufacturing. And it has to work for both.*

### Rule 2
### Relationship Conflict is Bad

> *How would you know? You're not a technical person.*
>
> *That's a stupid idea, Bob. You have no idea what you're talking about.*

If you're Bob, there's very little chance you'll ever speak your mind in a team meeting again. The next time, you'll probably just shut up. But the whole point of the team is to get the brightest minds to focus on a problem and create a solution. That means people will probably disagree with each other before they can agree, and they must feel safe to do so.

## 6 THE VALUE OF CONFLICT

Think of conflict as dialogue, not as confrontation. Dialogue uses a normal tone of voice; a raised voice signals confrontation. Body language is relaxed or neutral for dialogue; it is defensive or hostile during a confrontation.

When presenting a contrary point of view, your choice of language is important.

**Do**

- Listen before you speak.
- Be diplomatic. That doesn't mean being wishy-washy. Be respectful, but firm.
- Choose your language carefully. In a disagreement, using "you" can quickly sound accusatory, even if you don't mean it that way. *You've got it all wrong.*
- Reframe the comment from your vantage point, using an "I" statement. *The way I see it, the calculations are based on incorrect assumptions.*

**Don't**

- Interrupt.
- Attack.
- Be sarcastic.
- Take your frustration out on another team member.

Above all, don't clam up and wait until after the meeting, or until the next meeting, to tell others what you really think. Put it on the table during the meeting right now.

**When you can't agree**

- Agree to disagree temporarily. Then get together, with or without the project manager, to try to arrive at a solution.
- Get a wider range of opinions. Go outside the team for more information.
- Make it your goal to come to agreement. This is not the time to be a diva and storm out if your point is not immediately accepted.

Sometimes personalities clash and get in the way of team performance. If a team seems ready to implode, Susan Wheelan's advice is to focus on the work.

"You don't have to like anyone on the team. It's not about them, it's about the work. So focus on the work."

> **Focus on the Work**
>
> The Chicago Bulls in their heyday were an unstoppable basketball team that became a legend. But stars Michael Jordan and Dennis Rodman, who were formidable together on the court, were polar opposites in their personalities. They probably didn't even like each other and weren't likely to hang out after a game. But they knew how to focus on the work. Their team made history, and they made personal fortunes.

## GETTING STUCK IN BAD CONFLICT

Sometimes teams do get stuck in conflict between people. When it happens, the hostility between team members can be uncomfortable for everyone, and the work of the team bogs down. Connie Kirby, an organizational development consultant, helped one such team in a consumer products company get past their personal difficulties.

"The group had polarized into conducting shouting matches at each other," Kirby recalls. "By the time I was brought in, things had deteriorated to the point that people couldn't even look at each other. The tension in the room was palpable."

During a three-day off-site meeting designed to accomplish some company business and get the team back on track, Kirby directed the team away from the personality conflicts and back onto the work.

Adonna Bowman, a member of that team, recalls the experience. "The first night was really tense. No one knew what to expect. We came into the room and each person had a stack of poker chips on the table at their place. Connie asked everyone in turn to introduce themselves and talk about their roles and responsibilities. The rule was, any time someone disagreed, or thought what someone said wasn't true, or if made them angry, they could throw a poker chip on the floor. By the time the evening was over, no one had any poker chips left. There were poker chips all over the place."

The next morning, everyone had their stack of poker chips again. Now, the group began to break up into small groups of two and three to address departmental work and then report back to the larger group. They also ate all their meals together.

"At the end of the second day," Bowman says, "everyone had some poker chips left. What started out as acrimonious, eventually became funny. By the end of the three days of working on team business, people saw that they shared the same issues and were trying to accomplish the same things."

But did it last? "Absolutely," says Bowman. "Once people were able to hear that they really cared about the same work issues, it absolutely carried over. We never had the same kind of problems again."

## WHEN NO ONE WANTS TO SPEAK UP

The reason you're on a team in the first place is that a better solution results when great minds think together. So if no one ever disagrees with anyone else, the solution will come from whoever spoke first—or the loudest—or even just spoke at all. If that's all the team can produce, why waste the human and financial resources?

Wheelan's work with one team uncovered unspoken disagreements among the members about their shared goals and the strategies for meeting the goals. Because members avoided disagreeing with each other, their work ground to a halt.

Her approach was to collect the different points of view and present them anonymously. That way the group could discuss them without anyone having to own the contradictory opinions.

"From that point on, they became a different team," she says. "They worked hard on getting the issues articulated," which they did with outside help, "and then they engaged in resolving the issues."

If you find yourself in a similar situation, here's what you can do.

- Ask the team leader specifically to solicit other points of view during a meeting.
- Tell the team leader your concerns privately ahead of time. Ask him or her to raise them anonymously at a meeting.
- Talk individually with other team members before a meeting to take the temperature of their reactions to your ideas.

## MAKING DECISIONS

As a team, you won't always agree. So how will you make decisions? Figuring out how you'll do this is an early and important job of the team. And yet it's usually left unaddressed until the team hits a roadblock. It's easy to talk about the work. But it's just as important to talk about your process—about how you will operate as a team.

Establishing team processes includes agreeing on things like

- how often the group will meet
- who will lead the meetings
- whether meetings will start on time
- how the group will communicate
- how the group will make decisions

How do you make decisions? Your team may come up with its own inventive solution, but here are a few choices.

You can decide

- by negotiation
- by a simple majority
- by a two-thirds vote
- by consensus
- by a consultative process—one person is the decision maker, but must be educated by the group to make an informed decision

The consensus approach is often considered the least desirable, because it takes only one person to veto an idea. Then the team compromises to please everyone, which may result in a less-than-ideal solution.

There is no one right answer on making team decisions. Each team needs to work out its own method. The trick is to establish the rules *before* you need them.

## NOT EVERYONE BELONGS ON A TEAM

Not everyone belongs on a team. Suppose the team functions well, with the exception of one person. This person consistently derails the team despite the best efforts of the group leader. In that case, the project leader should consider replacing that person so the group can get on with its work.

And what if *you* think you have the wrong skill set for the team? Speak up. Let your team leader know that you're willing, but you think you don't have the expertise for this project.

# 7

# Communications

*There's a profound difference between information and meaning.*
—Warren Bennis

On any given subject, there's enough information out there to fill up your hard drive, overload your filing cabinets, and take over the storage shed. And even if all this detail is fascinating to you, it's probably not as compelling to anyone else. When you're on a team, how much information is enough? How much is too much?

Communication is more art than science. It involves transferring information in a way that makes sense to your audience. Finding that tipping point between usable information and overwhelming data is an art, but it can be learned.

It may come as a surprise to learn that good communication starts with listening. You need to consider these questions.

- Who needs to know?
- What do they need to know?
- What is their frame of reference?
- Do they speak your technical lingo or is that a foreign language to them?

The only way to answer these questions is to ask. Assume nothing. And then listen closely to the answers.

Organizational consultant Connie Kirby likes to say there are three essential skills in communicating with your fellow team members, with management, and with the client: 1) listening, 2) listening, and 3) listening.

> *As I get older, I've learned to listen to people rather than accuse them of things.*
>
> —Po Bronson

Experts agree that face-to-face communication is preferable whenever possible. In person, you have the advantage of nonverbal signals such as body language and facial expressions. These instant feedback signals let you know if you're clear and making sense. Or if you're confusing. Or if you're boring them to tears.

First, figure out who you are talking to. Your target audience might include

- team members
- subteams
- team partners
- decision makers
- clients or customers
- management
- finance people

- regulatory agencies
- industry groups
- company employees
- media

Next, figure out what they need to know. This will vary with each audience. Here are some common questions they may want answered.

**Team members**

- What is my team supposed to do?
- By when do we have to do it?
- What is my role in the process?
- What are the other subteams doing?
- Are they on schedule?
- Who do we hand this off to?

**Customers**

- How is the project evolving?
- What stage are you in?
- Are you going to meet the deadline?
- Are you going to stay within the budget?
- Is there more information we can provide?

**Management**

- How is the project progressing?
- Will it deliver on time?
- Are there any problems?
- Are the original projections for money, equipment, and people still on target?
- If they have changed, why?

## GETTING A GOOD COMMUNICATIONS FLOW

Be prepared for some trial and error in getting your project communications to flow smoothly. The communications challenges on a large-scale project are different than those for a smaller, self-contained team. Let's assume the project is too large for everyone to meet together regularly. The project manager divides the group into subteams. Communications must flow in several directions.

1. Each subteam member must understand that subteam's role in the overall project. If you're not sure, ask your project team leader to review it at the next meeting. Ask questions until you understand.

2. Subteam members must maintain a good flow of information among themselves. They need to exchange information freely, ask questions and, if there are different points of view, test solutions with each other. The best place to hammer out differences is within the subteam, before the project gets handed off to the next group.

3. When the work moves from one subteam to another, the two subteams must be in contact before the handoff to provide each other with context. (Context means general information, not every last detail about what your team did.)

4. Other teams down the line must also be kept up to speed on developments. Whether they are in manufacturing, sales, or marketing, they'll need to know what decisions have been made, and why. If the project's original assumptions have changed, they will need to adapt their thinking. High-level summaries are sufficient for these groups.

5. Keep the next level of management apprised of how the team is doing. They will want to know if the project is sticking to its schedule and budget, and if any obstacles threaten to derail either one. They probably won't have the time or the interest to hear about the nitty-gritty of development.

6. Don't forget the client, the ultimate user. Keep your customer in the loop.

To make your communications more effective, ask your audiences—whether that's another subteam or management or the client—how they want to receive information. Pay attention to which methods get the best results. As noted earlier, face-to-face communication is the most effective, but you'll also want to have a paper trail to document your communications. For project phase wrap-ups, a well-written and documented report paves the way for the next phase, whether it's conducted by the same team or a different one. It also provides an ongoing record of your work.

## AVOIDING OVERLOAD

Steve Winshel, an experienced executive who has managed many project teams, says that the trick is to get information flowing up, down, and across.

"The classic mistake is to have walls between internal technology groups, so one group doesn't know what the other group is doing. The design group and the coding group—they need to be communicating with each other, but not every little nit." Guidance from the team leader can help team members understand what is enough and what is too much.

Donald Apy began his career as a product development engineer in New England. He eventually moved to Silicon Valley, where he worked as a software engineer, a project lead, and ultimately as manager of an IT development group. He recalls one sprawling product development team that was divided into subteams.

"You can easily get information overload with such a large group," he says. "Initially, people from other subteams were sending out these giant status emails, and you had no idea if there was something in them that pertained to you. Maybe 80 percent of the way through you'd find something. But eventually people just started ignoring them, because it was too much work to sort through all that irrelevant information."

The solution came with guidance from the project manager, who coached team members on how to create targeted messages. Detailed information was circulated only within the subteam. What went to the other subteams were highlights. "Even then," says Apy, "the targeted communications required a summary at the top, which helped everyone access the information they needed, and discard the rest."

## VIRTUAL TEAMS

One of Donald Apy's project teams spanned the world. With members in the United States from both the Pacific and Mountain time zones, one member in Australia, another in Ireland, and yet another in the United Kingdom, team meetings across time zones were a way of life.

"It is challenging, so everyone has to be little flexible," Apy says. "For one-on-ones with people in the U.K. and Ireland, I got up at 5:30 in the morning. Australia wasn't a problem, because I could do that at the end of the business day. But having entire team meetings was harder. We rotated the time of the meeting to distribute the pain about who wakes up early and who stays up late, and who gets to attend during their regular business hours.

"In this case, the person in Australia was a night owl, which worked out great for the group. It eliminated some of the pain. And because the meetings were conference calls, people could attend from home, depending on the time."

---

**Selling Your Ideas**

Sometimes the communications challenges are unexpected, as in the case of this project team with a relatively simple structure.

Fredric Laurentine led a quality improvement team for a Silicon Valley technology company. Dubbed the First Encounter Team, its job was to improve the customer's experience with the product. Over a period of eight months, this team traveled to customer sites in the United States, Europe, and Asia to meet with customers and learn firsthand why customers said the equipment was both hard to set up and hard to use.

The team's members represented manufacturing, sales, marketing, industrial design, operations, and quality departments. All had regular ongoing responsibilities and had volunteered to participate on the team in addition to their normal duties. Communication among team members was straightforward because the group was relatively small. They traveled together and observed the customer's difficulties together. They had meetings at which every member was present.

As the team traveled, they discovered that what made the product difficult to use was a series of what Laurentine describes as "Enormous Silly Problems"—things that, on the surface, seemed minor, but in fact were very important.

"People had pet ideas about why customers said the equipment was hard to use. Some would say we needed to color-code the cables because they're not easy to hook up. That was not the problem. Others said we needed to improve the documentation. In fact, we learned that very few people even opened the documentation; most just stacked it up in the corner. So, improving documentation was not a good way to improve usability."

Because the team included representatives from every key department involved with the product, it was able to learn a great deal about why the problem existed. "There is a saying that your next problem is caused by your last solution. We found that the majority of the problems were caused by the way the equipment was packed," says Laurentine. "Customers found it confusing to open the boxes and set up the equipment when it arrived because the boxes weren't marked. We discovered that product was shipped in boxes without descriptions, because unmarked boxes kept down box inventories at the factories. That was a good thing when volume was low, but it made no sense when product volume soared and boxes were being replenished on a daily basis.

"We also learned that one size didn't fit all customers. U.S. customers preferred to receive the product in pallets of components, while German customers wanted giant boxes of complete systems."

The solution was as simple as identifying the contents on the outside of the box and including a configuration checker to make sure the customer had ordered a complete system.

The team's client in this case was upper management. The communications challenge turned out to be convincing management to take their findings seriously. "The initial response generally went something like, 'Oh, that's so simple, I can't believe it's a problem,' and they'd move on to the next issue," says Laurentine. "It took relentless presentations and explanations from every team member's perspective, supported by documentation in the form of photographs and interviews, to persuade them."

PROFESSIONAL PUBLICATIONS, INC.

## REPETITION

*The greatest problem in communication is the illusion that it has been accomplished.*

—George Bernard Shaw

Your project team has been living with the work for some time. It's easy to forget that others haven't. Even though you communicate periodically with various groups about your progress, always include a summary of what you've already told them up to this point. The summary provides context for your latest information. They'll appreciate the reminder.

## COMMUNICATING WITH THE CLIENT

Working with clients is a skill to be cultivated.

On many teams there may be one or more members who are in direct contact with the client. Sometimes it's the team leader. Sometimes it is a designated member. The client may be an external customer or an internal department. Or it may be a regulatory agency or legal counsel.

Teams that really get involved in their work naturally want to build the best possible solutions. But there is the reality of budgets that don't always allow for making the best thing. Or the reality that consumers may find your incredible product far too difficult to use. Or perhaps your "best" solution doesn't meet the regulatory standards.

Keep your team on track by getting regular feedback from the people in touch with your clients. Nothing is more discouraging than to devise the world's most ingenious mousetrap, complete with electronic sensors and digital readouts, only to find that the client really just wants another version of the old spring-loaded kind. Chances are, not only is your client unwilling to pay for the best possible mousetrap, he also doesn't want to figure out how to use your brilliant but complicated version. It won't matter how brilliant the solution is if the client rejects it.

### Understanding the Client

Parnian Kaboli has been a civil engineer, then a geotechnical engineer, and now an environmental engineer. In her experience as a project leader, her work has often brought her into contact with in-house counsel, external counsel, and regulatory agencies.

In one case, she had to manage a project team comprised of several PhDs and four or five field engineers. Yet she also had to reach agreement for the team's approach from the legal experts who were her ultimate clients.

"I discovered that very few engineers really understand the Superfund Law, but they have to follow its regulations on the project site. It means working with legal counsel, both inside and externally. Counsel has their own way of handling things. By paying close attention, I came to understand how the lawyers work, and how the regulators work.

"Every interaction with the lawyers or the regulators was the same as negotiating a deal," Kaboli says. "You might be an environmental engineer dealing with limits and test results, and yet, you are negotiating a business deal."

## UNOFFICIAL COMMUNICATIONS

Even when you're not working on a project for a client, it's still a good idea to keep client departments informed of new developments and technologies of interest. Technology transfer should always take place.

Reports, minutes of committee meetings, and trip reports, for example, can be routinely channeled to appropriate departmental contacts. Keeping your client and others informed of what you and your team are doing will prove immensely valuable. Good project team players become known, and are usually well received the next time they come before upper management to propose another project.

## CLOSE ENCOUNTERS

In his book, *What a Great Idea*, Charles Thompson illustrates how Steelcase, a manufacturer of office furniture, promoted communications between various departments by creating an innovative office layout. The new design created a corporate geography that required finance to mingle with sales, with product design, and with advertising. This clustered layout brought people together physically, and ultimately intellectually as well. Proximity produces an intermingling of ideas and problem solving.

The Steelcase layout created a natural opportunity to talk and share intelligence. Only so much happens in formal meetings; people frequently reveal themselves more readily in a casual setting. There's an unforced communications flow you get when you're in the same location. What you overhear while getting coffee often gives more insight into what's actually going on than you get in official interviews.

# 8

# Cultivating Creativity

*Creativity is the generation of novel ideas. Innovation is making money with these ideas.*
—Harry T. Roman

Creativity is like humor: The more you try to analyze it, the more elusive it becomes.

It's easier to describe the conditions in which creativity thrives than to define it. Teams work best in an open and free environment. Even if your corporate culture doesn't welcome an exchange of ideas, teams can create their own mini-cultures. Team members must be able to challenge the status quo. The fewer restrictions there are, the more creativity flourishes.

For years, experts have tried to measure creativity. At best, they have developed some models and guidelines. But there are no scientific measurements, only indicators of its potential.

## ARE YOU CREATIVE?

Here are some indicators of creativity.

- Creative people interact with other people. Scientists and engineers who interact frequently with their peers tend to be more innovative.
- Good interpersonal skills, especially in oral and written communications, are an advantage.
- Creativity often involves working on both the conscious and subconscious levels. Combining knowledge with imagination, logic, and intuition leads to new ideas.
- Jobs themselves may not be creative, but the setting or environment is a strong influence on the creative ability of the person performing the job.
- Creative people do not judge ideas until they've made a thorough analysis of their value.

Creative group sessions are 10 to 12 times more productive than one person working alone. Brainstorming feeds off ideas.

If you're lucky enough to be able to select your team members, you can tap people you know are creative. But creativity alone doesn't guarantee a successful outcome. You still have to translate the idea into something that works in the marketplace.

Here's more about creative people.

- Creative people are highly motivated, independent, and persistent in their attempts to find solutions.
- They have a well-developed sense of humor.
- They are flexible in the way they think.
- They vary their approaches to problems.
- Creative people are often well read in any number of areas. They have a diverse knowledge base from which to generate ideas.
- They have varied interests and are open to new ideas and experiences. In childhood they had a wide range of interests.
- They accept ambiguity and uncertainty in their search for solutions to problems.

- They tend to savor the complex and novel over the conventional and symmetrical.
- The creative manager is a perfectionist.
- Creative team members are capable of added responsibility, but often do not desire it.

Choreographer Twyla Tharp argues that creativity is a habit. By cultivating good work habits, she says, you are more likely to access creative ideas.

## EIGHT STEPS TO CREATIVITY

The following is a tried and true way to foster creativity.

1. Start with a real need, application, or problem.
2. Establish a creative environment in which to work on the problem.
3. Change your viewpoint. Look at the problem from different angles and perspectives. It's a given that you'll think about the technical considerations. But have you or your teammates considered the problem or idea from these other aspects?
    - environment
    - political
    - institutional
    - legal
    - technical
    - regulatory
    - economic
    - social
4. Concentrate on the need. Persist in your desire to solve the problem.
5. Let go of the idea that you must think of something novel. Pore over old files. Looking at previous research or projects by colleagues might just trigger an idea for your project. Talk to people with lots of experience. They know more than they've ever put down on paper.

6. Give your ideas time to marinate—don't judge them too quickly.
7. Refine and revisit your ideas—this is the time to judge.
8. Apply your ideas to workable solutions.

> *Innovators learn that it's better to ask for forgiveness than for permission.*
>
> —3M website

Some questions to push your thinking in new directions.

- How else could we use this?
- What else could be made from this?
- What other uses might there be if we modified this?

And the biggest one—

- What if?

---

**Team Creativity Exercise**

Set up a debate. Pick two or more potential solutions. Assign each one to one or several team members to argue the position.

Really go at it. See what happens when you get into the argument. This can shatter barriers and take your thinking to new levels.

# 9

# Beyond Technical Knowledge

*The ability to deal with the customer as a client is just as important as the technical end of problem solving.*

—Elliott Ross

A hot project is getting under way, and you'd like to be part of it. Let's say there are several people who have the same technical skill set as you. How do you rise above the crowd to be the one chosen as an asset to the team?

If there's a choice, the team leader will choose the one who brings something extra. Your contribution to the team can be much greater than your technical skills alone.

Here are a few of the most valued attributes you can bring to the team. Incidentally, they're also great attributes for team leaders, too. These qualities help any team achieve better results.

## THINKING LIKE THE CLIENT

Getting inside the head of your client or customer is crucial to your team's success. This is about more than simply the trust a client has placed in you and the team. It involves understanding the client's environment.

Expect each client to have different priorities. Ask yourself these questions.

- What are their priorities?
- What factors affect their operations?

An operating department responsible for keeping equipment and machinery functioning day after day will have different needs than one responsible for regional sales offices or corporate accounting. The best way to learn about your client's needs is to spend time on location or with a department contact.

This will do several things.

- You'll gain insight into the problem.
- You'll get a truer perspective on the department's culture.
- People will get to know you. They'll recognize you as concerned and interested.

Spending time with your client is an excellent way to learn how he or she thinks. You'll build new working relationships and renew old ones. And ultimately, your team's work will be more effective. You'll be able to define and articulate the client department's needs.

Just as important, you will be able to forecast the cost of your project with greater precision. When you're pitching management to invest in it, you'll know what you're talking about.

## THE C WORD

Commitment.

Sure, you have specific responsibilities within the project. But team leaders are looking for more than that. They look for people with the capacity to make a deep commitment to the project.

- Are you dedicated to finding the best solution for the situation?
- Do you show up to meetings on time?
- Do you contribute ideas or wait for someone else to go first?
- Do you give honest feedback?
- Are you available to help other team members?
- Do you push to meet schedules and deliverables?
- Do you think about the project when you don't have to?
- Do you respect the work?
- Do people like working with you?

## COMMUNICATION SKILLS

Teams live and die by their ability to sell their thoughts, ideas, and concepts, not only to each other but to client departments, management, and others. Good oral and written communication skills are an asset for any team member.

Oral presentations are the usual way you will communicate. Edit your ideas and your words before presenting them. Don't wing it.

If you're not comfortable making presentations, look for opportunities to practice that won't have an impact on your career. Check out your company's professional and skill development programs as possibilities. In most metropolitan areas you can find evening courses in presentation skills at area schools and colleges.

## SUSPEND JUDGMENT

Allow some quiet time to think about the project and new ideas. It's so easy to toss out a new idea prematurely. Let new ideas cook for a while before you pass judgment. Have several colleagues examine them. Group creativity can be productive, much more so than a single individual's efforts. Try using the project team as a springboard for new ideas.

## BE ASSERTIVE

Once you have your assignment and understand your responsibilities, become an active participant on the team. You may observe opportunities for taking the idea further, to refine the solution. Speak up. Lobby for the best solution for the customer.

## PERSISTENCE

*It's not that I'm so smart, it's just that I stay with problems longer.*
—Albert Einstein

Creativity is the tool that puts you on the road to innovation. But your team's new idea still must be marketed and sold. Whether for a client department or an external customer, the idea must hold up under the scrutiny of the user.

Your ability to sell the idea is a key factor in its success. Don't be surprised if your team's idea is received coolly at first. Initial rejections are not unusual. Persistence might be the single biggest factor in transforming creative ideas into innovations that become marketplace successes.

If your idea is not understood the first time around, don't give up. Maybe you haven't presented it in the best light. Maybe people need to hear it more than once.

---

**Sticking With It**

Here is a great example of how success can come from apparent failure. And it's an amazing story about how a few persistent people made it happen.

When a 3M research scientist inadvertently developed an adhesive that could be repositioned and still stick, he was really looking for a different, stronger adhesive. Even though his original attempt failed, everyone knows the happy end of this story—the invention of Post-it Notes, a new communications medium that changed the way we leave messages, write notes, and highlight passages.

But the 12 years it took from discovery to marketing shows the value of persistence. At first, the inventor was a lone voice, touting the merits of the new adhesive to anyone in the company who would listen. It was five years before he found a champion.

Even then, another five years went by before another 3M employee stumbled onto the perfect application. A new-product researcher was frustrated when the scraps of paper he used to mark pages in his choir book kept falling out. He remembered the adhesive, and a sticky bookmark was born.

Many other applications soon followed. But even then, these persistent champions encountered resistance from engineering, production, and market research. It took an experimental sales effort with management in tow, walking up and down the streets of Richmond, Virginia, to prove that people would readily buy the product.

The rest, as winners like to say, is history. Without the remarkable persistence of a few people, the research scientist would have filed away the formula in the "Failed" file.

# 10

# Assembling Resources

*I'm a great believer in luck, and I find the harder I work the more I have of it.*

—Thomas Jefferson

Have you considered all the resources available to your team? Every new contact can contribute more insight toward your solution.

Some of the resources outlined in this chapter are essential to every team. Others may not be required on every project. As your team gets up and running, look over the list. Some may turn out to be unexpected sources of additional funding. Volunteer to organize some resources that are a good fit with your knowledge and capabilities.

# RESOURCES

Resources come in many forms.

- human talent and motivation
- technology
- contacts within and outside the corporation
- vendors, developers, and researchers
- academic expertise
- professional organizations
- related industries
- conferences, symposia, workshops, and professional forums
- federal and state agencies
- the international community

## Human Talent and Motivation

The talent assembled within the team seems almost too obvious to mention. But talent without motivation usually leaves a team wanting more. Motivated team members add a special sizzle to a team. So don't overlook this essential resource.

And don't forget the hidden skills each employee brings to the job. People have interests outside of work. Learn about your fellow team members and their interests. There just might be a serendipitous match between one member's outside interests and the team's needs.

## Technology

Technology is the foundation of innovation. It's the tool you use to create new products and services. Because it changes and evolves, make sure you have access to the latest technology within the company. If not, you may need to recruit an outside consultant or specialist to supply essential expertise to the team.

The impact of the technology will be important, too. The team should have people who understand how the technology will influence the users of the products and services you create.

## Contacts Within and Outside the Corporation

Experienced project engineers know the truth of the saying: "It's not *what* you know but *who* you know that counts."

Information is a precious commodity. If you know where to get information, inside or outside the company, you become an indispensable resource. Members of the team use every scrap of knowledge they have to locate information relevant to their work.

In our professional lives, the information and contact networks we develop over our careers fuel our success. When members of the team pool their contacts and information sources, they increase the wealth of the team. A good project engineer will organize a database for easy access and retrieval.

It may be appropriate for some team members see firsthand what other companies have done in similar areas. Be prepared to travel. Face-to-face communication is effective. New product development, in particular, is a human process. This builds the contact base of the team and directly transfers information and new technology.

And don't forget the company library. There may be untold information in the files, books, and search engines.

## Vendors, Developers, and Researchers

No one team knows it all. Many external sources can be tapped for their expertise. Vendors and developers are often an excellent source of information about what has been tested and proven not to work. This kind of intelligence can save you from false starts and wasting resources. Vendors and developers are also future potential investors in your products and services. View them as potential partners.

In addition to being great sources of information, vendors often design their products specifically for an industry's market. They might be eager to work with industry representatives to test, refine, and demonstrate their technology. An astute project team can capture this enthusiasm through low-cost joint projects with vendors.

PROFESSIONAL PUBLICATIONS, INC.

In exchange for the use or rental of a vendor's equipment, you might agree to share field test data. This can be a win-win arrangement for both of you. The vendor gets an economical test laboratory. And you get to use equipment without having to actually purchase it. You never know when it will also help stimulate future product developments.

Several team members might join with one or more vendors to create product user groups that meet regularly to share technology and ideas. Vendors need to see a marketplace for their products. Project managers need to know what is available. By working together, both parties benefit.

Researchers and others who operate in advanced areas are also valuable resources. These professionals can give the team a glimpse of where technology is headed and how your new products and services may evolve over time. If you are fortunate enough to have researchers within your company who can provide guidance, seriously consider inviting them to join your team. People from a variety of backgrounds and disciplines add to the reach and impact of a team.

### Academic Expertise

This can be a unique resource. Like researchers, academics expand the boundaries of known technology and experience. Their freedom to explore often means they have collected knowledge from a wide variety of sources, while their own research creates new information. This can become an asset to your team.

Graduate and undergraduate students are also an excellent source of talent. Students can sometimes perform their academic projects and thesis work in areas that are directly relevant to the team's needs. More and more, colleges and universities urge their professors and students to work closely with the industrial community.

### Professional Organizations

Here is an often overlooked source of information for the hungry team. Most professional organizations have vast communications networks. Mine them. Your team members most likely belong to professional organizations and can

# 10 ASSEMBLING RESOURCES — 69

tap into these databases directly. Large industry groups can offer tremendous insight into technology directly related to your work.

## Related Industries

Sister industries may be exploring related avenues. They may be trying to develop products and services similar to your own efforts.

Except for issues of proprietary research, these related industries may be willing to join forces with you and leverage their resources along with yours. Explore this opportunity to magnify the effect of your work and maximize precious financial resources. Make sure you don't duplicate what others are already doing. At the very least, share lessons learned in the process.

## Conferences and Symposia

If your team's work is new and unique, you probably won't find much that's helpful in a textbook. Instead, look for articles in industry journals, and papers from professional conferences and workshops.

Your team should be prepared to attend these sessions and integrate these findings into the project. This information can often be of immediate value. In many cases, it is the only reputable source of information.

## Government Agencies

Federal and state agencies are increasingly willing to work with industry and corporations on joint projects. Sometimes agencies have funds available to underwrite the development of new products and services. Like sister industries, when projects can be relevant to the public at large, federal and state agencies are a way to leverage resources.

## The International Community

Competition isn't the only thing becoming global. So is cooperation. International partnerships are becoming commonplace. The international technical community has always been an open forum, which can directly benefit your team's efforts.

## FINDING FINANCIAL RESOURCES

In many cases, the decision to fund a project will have been made at the highest management levels. But in those instances where you are directly responsible for finding funding for your project, there is a range of places you can look.

Typically, funds are available at two levels: from your department, and through the overall corporate budget as a specific line item. Consider dividing large complex projects into discrete tasks that could be funded independently by various departments within the same company. How this works will vary with the size of the company you work for and with the size of the project. Learn how the system works in your organization. Ask for the necessary paperwork. Use every team member to develop the necessary justification.

If a project seems tenuous at the outset, break it into smaller phases over time. Budget each phase separately to avoid losing the whole project. Don't forget to give upper management the ability to review the team's work regularly. It keeps your project visible.

A real signal of a successful collaboration is when the client department contributes its own funds to the project and visibly commits its own resources.

Here are some more options for financial resources.

### David-and-Goliath Partnerships

Large companies often invest venture capital in smaller, nimbler companies. This is common among global pharmaceutical companies, which invest in the exploratory work of small biotech firms. Even some of the largest companies with deep resources collaborate with each other. Apple Computer, for example, collaborates with Hewlett-Packard and Motorola on a variety of new products and applications.

## 10 ASSEMBLING RESOURCES  71

### Venture Capital

Don't rule out the pure venture capital firms, many of which have specific niches in which they invest. Investors, entrepreneurs, and others may provide funding or in-kind services that can give your team an added financial boost. This is especially pertinent when a project involves the development of radically new technology or a stark departure from traditional new products/service development.

### Your Internal Finance Group

To make sure you have all the right players on the team, don't forget to involve your corporate financial people. Their role goes beyond just forking over money when you need it. They can be important allies in your work.

Most delays in getting money approved for a project happen when key people don't understand what you are doing. Keep people informed, especially your financial people. They can be invaluable when it comes to classifying how your project funds are to be allocated and charged against your work.

This is not trivial. If the team is working on cutting-edge ideas, there may not be a way to account for the expenditures incurred. Suppose you do find external funding to offset costs. Is there a traditional way to treat these outside sources of revenue? Having the team meet regularly with the financial people early and often helps set up proper procedures. Make them part of the team.

---

**Involving Your Finance Group**

Harry T. Roman says, "I can testify firsthand to the importance of involving corporate financial people in a project. While trying to authorize almost $2 million in funding for the development of new robotic hardware, it became obvious that our financial people were having difficulty in deciding how to treat the expenses. Should they be capitalized or left as operating charges?

"To prove my point about the need for capitalization expenses, I took the financial group out in the field to see some of my robotic devices in action. They operated the robots and saw their capabilities firsthand. I not only proved my

---

PROFESSIONAL PUBLICATIONS, INC.

point, I made several new friends in the company and saved my team several months' waiting time. We delivered new robots to our client departments on time and on budget.

"The most rewarding part occurred when one of the members of the financial group remarked that he had been approving authorizations for over thirty years, and this was the first time he actually went into the field to see the equipment. He told me he would be doing that a lot more now."

### Purchasing and Contracts

The expertise within the in-house purchasing, contract, and legal groups is a valuable resource and worth exploring. If you involve outside companies and vendors in the team, there may be important proprietary concerns involved with the technology they bring. Working agreements will need to be developed, as well as patents and copyrights. Everyone's interests must be protected—most of all the client department's. Everything you and the team do and accomplish reflects upon the client department.

## PUBLICIZING YOUR TEAM

The more people know about your team and its work, the more momentum you build. Publicity is your ally—especially with key audiences—as long as you are not revealing confidential information. It keeps your team's work in the forefront and can actually attract other resources, including potential partners and supporters.

It is also essential that others within the company know of your work, since they may have something to contribute. And it is always important to keep management up to date on the team's progress.

Think of it as marketing and publicizing your project, separate from the formal project communications discussed in Ch. 7. It often pays unexpected benefits. When marketing or advertising your team's work,

- always keep key people and the general population of your company informed of your progress and findings
- make sure significant advances and events are shared with the client department

Remember who you are working for. Share the limelight with them.

Keep the outside world apprised of your activities. This applies especially to outside supporters like consultants and vendors, and outside agencies that are potential sources of funding. Keeping them aware of what you're doing could attract support for your work.

## INTERNAL MARKETING

There are a number of ways to advertise and market your team's work. And you won't need a big budget to do it. Here are just some of the methods you might consider to communicate the results of your work within your company. Most of these are relatively low in cost.

- Write an article for your company newspaper or magazine.
- Give presentations to
    - senior management
    - client department
    - other interested departments
- Host demos of your technology.
- Develop a low-cost bulletin board type of display.
- Publish a low-cost pamphlet or flyer describing your work.
- Host a technology transfer seminar for your company's technical staff.
- Hands-on demonstrations are always fun to do if your work lends itself to it, as in the robot demonstrations mentioned earlier in this chapter.

## EXTERNAL PUBLICITY

There are equally effective ways to market and publicize results to the outside world, such as magazine articles and technical papers. A single well-done article or paper can easily generate 10 or 20 inquiries about your work from interested outside parties. An article in a prominent newspaper can produce a snowstorm of inquiries if the right audience is tapped. Both of these have ongoing value, as you can send reprints to agencies, vendors, and researchers to build more interest.

If your work has produced proprietary results, you may not want to disclose detailed information to the public. It's good practice to consider all outside communication to be public disclosure. Communication with the outside world is a double-edged sword, but if handled with care it can produce some amazing new working relationships.

Here are some ways to communicate results externally.

**Publish articles in**

- magazines
- journals
- industry newsletters

**Give presentations at**

- industry conferences and seminars
- key industry committee meetings
- technical society meetings
- offices of funding agencies

**Contact science and technology editors at**

- newspapers
- magazines
- newsletters

**Work with vendors to develop**

- a display
- a joint marketing effort

Regardless of where you communicate your results, be sure to do so within the guidelines set up by your company. If the work will be discussed outside the company, it should be cleared

- by the team
- by the client
- by management
- by your company's public information department

The public information people are professionals who can set up media contacts for you. They can give guidance on how to act in an interview. They also can help you avoid potentially embarrassing pitfalls. They are a valuable asset to you and your team.

When you publicize your team's results, include photos of team members along with client department personnel to show that the work is truly a collaborative effort.

## EMPHASIZE RESULTS

In every medium, focus on what the team has accomplished. Then project what is planned next. It shows your readers you are action oriented.

Use your company's communications network to announce important events and exhibitions. Consider inviting selected individuals to attend your meetings.

If your project is a long one, covering two or more years, consider communicating results on a yearly basis. Create your own annual report on the project, and give copies to your client, management, and other external supporters. When your project is finished, issue a wrap-up of the entire effort.

# 11

# Some Special Teams

Whether inside the walls of a company or in the field on special assignment, a team is still a team. The following accounts are from teams who volunteered for special assignments, and they give an interesting view into how a team works in unusual circumstances.

## DOCUMENTING THE TSUNAMI: TWO PERSPECTIVES

After a natural disaster, teams of senior engineers will often volunteer to assess the extent and impact of the damage firsthand. Their observations of physical destruction and summaries of lessons learned add important information to the body of knowledge for engineers everywhere.

Engineers generally volunteer under the auspices of the American Society of Civil Engineering (ASCE) or the Earthquake Engineering Research Institute (EERI). In particular, ASCE's institutes and technical committees, such as the Technical Council on Lifeline and Earthquake Engineering (TCLEE) and the Coasts, Oceans, Ports, and Rivers Institute (COPRI), are the organizing groups.

Organizing time is short. Teams must be assembled quickly. One month after the earthquake and tsunami that devastated parts of India and Southeast Asia in late 2004, three cross-functional teams of professional engineers from various disciplines came to India, Thailand, and Sri Lanka to document the disaster. Each team was a blend of first-time volunteers and experienced investigators. Here is a glimpse into their experiences.

## An Experienced View

TCLEE has a long tradition of dispatching teams of volunteer engineers to document and assess earthquake damage. Since the Loma Prieta earthquake in California in 1989, Curt Edwards, PE, has led volunteer teams to assess earthquake damage in locations as far-flung as India, Turkey, and Algeria. In his work life, Edwards is vice president of Pountney Psomas, a San Diego-based civil engineering firm.

With about a dozen team trips under his belt, Edwards' process is well established. As the chair of TCLEE's Earthquake Investigations Committee, he maintains an email distribution list of some 40 engineers who are potential volunteers. "We have training meetings periodically, so that people know what to do when they're in the field."

TCLEE typically coordinates with volunteers from EERI, and from the U.K.-based International Civil Engineering (ICE). To assess the effects of the tsunami, TCLEE invited COPRI to send volunteers with expertise in ocean and port damage. Edwards helped organize three international teams for ASCE and led the team going to Thailand.

"The hardest part is picking the dates, finding times that work for volunteers who have work schedules. There's a fine line between going too early and going too late. Typically we wait from three to five weeks after the event. We're there to document infrastructure damage. If you go too soon, things are still

## 11  SOME SPECIAL TEAMS

chaotic, and you can't meet with the people you need to see. But, if you wait too long, then things are all covered up, and you don't get photos of damage. Because this is all volunteer work, it's good for all of us to all be there at same time and coordinate the effort.

"Once you get the dates, you can start working on the physical arrangements. Are there hotels still available to be lived in? When we went to India, all the hotels were unusable. We ended up making arrangements, through ASCE's Washington D.C. representative, with the American Red Cross. We stayed in the Red Cross encampment in a tent."

Edwards generally coordinates with engineering universities in the host country because they're interested in the team's work. It's also a likely place to find engineers who speak English. In Thailand, the local university provided a 10-person van for the team.

"Often, we take a day to drive around the damage area and get the logistics," Edwards said. "How long does it take us to get there? Are the freeways open? Can we drive? Then, when we get back, we work out a plan for where we need people to go, and break into smaller teams.

"Typically we meet in the evening. In Thailand, everybody was back by 9 P.M., so we'd meet down in the lobby." As team leader, Edwards says he would ask team members, "'What'd you do today? Did you finish? Do you want to go somewhere else?' We didn't have time for people to be going to the same places.

"You can work like this intensely for about four days: Get up at 6 A.M., have breakfast, get going at daybreak, come back at 6 or 8 at night, have your meeting at 9, go to bed at 11. Then you get up the next day and do it all over again on five or six hours of sleep."

As team leader, Edwards usually stayed up and entered notes on the computer. "It's a pretty intense four days, but I'm finding that four days is usually enough. You start getting burned out, and you pretty much get all data you can get. We always try to take a fifth day of R&R before we come home." Including travel, the trip usually lasts from seven to nine days.

The data gathered by the team forms the basis of monograph reports, which are published by ASCE. For the Indian tsunami and Sumatran earthquake, ASCE has given the group permission to publish reports on a webpage. "It's a working document—we can make additions and corrections to it as it goes along. Hopefully the data will be seen by more people that way," Edwards says.

Typically, universities buy the books and reports. Team members give presentations and occasional seminars to professional organizations, including the local chapters of ASCE and the American Public Works Association. TCLEE has its own conference every three years, for which people are writing papers.

The real value of the team investigations is a continued emphasis on prevention. "We just keep hammering on what you have to do. It happens after every earthquake, and it will happen after the tsunami, too. No matter how horrible it was, in five years it will be just a distant memory. You'll see the same shoddy construction practices start coming back because they're cheaper."

## A First-Time Experience

John Headland, PE, is a principal of Moffatt & Nichol, a firm specializing in the planning and design of infrastructure and facilities around waterfronts. He is also a member of the COPRI board, and had urged COPRI to participate in volunteer activities similar to those of TCLEE.

"TCLEE has a practice of doing it for earthquakes, and I thought COPRI had an obligation to our members to enlighten people on what happens. After the tsunami, TCLEE approached us to accompany them on their trip. Because I was an advocate that COPRI should get involved in this type of activity, the COPRI board said, 'Good. You're in charge.'

"We had only about two weeks to get ready, and we followed the logistical lead of the TCLEE group. They had already gotten to work on determining how many people were going and to what countries. COPRI wanted to include Indonesia, because that's where most of fatalities occurred, but the political situation just wasn't conducive.

"I asked for volunteers and made recommendations about who should represent COPRI, based on their expertise. Ultimately ASCE and the COPRI board made the decision about whether we had the right groups. We wanted people familiar with ports and coastal flooding on each team. In the case of the

## 11  SOME SPECIAL TEAMS

Thailand team, the expertise of those two COPRI members was more heavily weighted toward coastal issues."

Headland's recommendations included two professors, one an authority on coastal engineering and the other an expert on ships and ports from the Naval Academy. Also tapped was a senior structural engineer for the Port of Los Angeles.

The Sri Lankan team organized their daily expeditions based on local conditions.

"Originally, we had ambitions of doing things on our own, but when we got on the ground, we realized how long a drive it all was," Headland said. "TCLEE had arranged for a bus, and we decided we'd better bunk with them. That worked out well.

"It's remarkable how different a prism each of us viewed the damage through. COPRI engineers looked at the effects of the action of the sea, whether it was knocking down buildings, or in the case of bridges, looking at the effects of erosion and scour. TCLEE engineers, because they're seismic and structural engineers, were interested in the bridge itself, and the effects from shaking of the ground."

The local contact came through a TCLEE member originally from Sri Lanka. "His brother, a local businessman in Colombo, knew the area backwards and forwards. So he arranged for the bus that would carry us around. He knew ahead of time which hotels were open and available and set that up.

"When it came to where we went, we simply got on the bus in Colombo and drove along the coast. Once you got on the road and saw what had happened, it was pretty clear when you needed to stop and look at specific sites.

"Our group included four engineers from TCLEE, two of us from COPRI, and one from the Institute of Civil Engineers (ICE), the British equivalent of ASCE. We were grateful for the three Sri Lankans who accompanied us—TCLEE's U.S. connection, and his brother and sister-in-law, who served as our guides and translators. We had two drivers.

"We were driving in the bus for 14 hours or more every day. We'd get out to take pictures and measure things. They were long days, but our time on the bus was productive. We had plenty of time together, so we would talk through issues, and discuss what we thought cause and effect was at one site or another. There was a lot of cross-education, because some our colleagues had not seen ocean-related things in the past, and we talked a lot about that from the COPRI side of things. We drew a lot of conclusions on the bus."

## What the Team Learned

"The first priority is, get basic safety, food, and shelter straightened out. You've got to have reliable people on the ground, reliable transportation, and you must avoid difficult places. You can step on something and get a cut. There could be disease. Just those basic things, that's first.

"Then the second thing, even though it seems so obvious, is to set up a reasonable itinerary so the team can see what needs to be seen and see it with enough time. In Sri Lanka, we were really pushing it. We covered over 500 miles in four days of driving on tough roads. Having reliable people on the ground made a big difference."

Local connections were a huge asset. Through links from colleagues in Moffat & Nichol's New York office, the team made a connection with someone who worked for the Sri Lankan Hydraulic Institute. "He arranged all our meetings with port officials, with a professor of coastal engineering at the local university, and with the Coastal Zone management group," Headland says. "We also had a connection to several local agencies, including the Port Authority of Sri Lanka, which is the government coastal planning group.

"Through ASCE and ICE, one night we met with the local ICE chapter of Sri Lanka, some 20-plus people. I think the whole team attended that meeting. We debated and talked, which was so important, because you don't get the right perspective if you haven't talked to the local people. In Sri Lanka, they were wrestling with an edict by the government to rebuild or put up new construction, depending on whether they were 100 or 200 meters back from shoreline—which meant massive upheaval.

"Because of our local connections, we didn't run into any cultural barriers. In fact, despite their tragic circumstances, the people were so friendly and open, and just drew us in. We made some good friends in Sri Lanka."

The team's results included presentations at COPRI-sponsored conferences on coastal disasters, as well as special conference sessions and papers on each country. The COPRI members are preparing a special COPRI report and contributing pieces to the TCLEE report.

## AFTER THE HURRICANE

Eight months after returning from Sri Lanka, Headland joined an ASCE-sponsored New Orleans levee assessment team following Hurricane Katrina in summer 2005. Along with Tony Dalrymple, a professor at Johns Hopkins and the COPRI team leader, other COPRI team members included an engineer from Japan and a professor of engineering from Holland. They were joined by engineers from ASCE's Geo-Institute and the National Science Foundation.

Headland says, "It was a completely different experience from Sri Lanka, as the Corps of Engineers pinpointed every site for us. We followed them around in cars we rented in Baton Rouge. We looked at sites where there were levee breaches, including the 17th Street, London, and Industrial canals, and to sites along the Gulf Intercoastal Waterway. One day we went by boat to sites along the Mississippi River Gulf outlet because it was the only way to gain access to the levees."

"One of the major differences, from a technical perspective, was that a tsunami is unexpected. In Sri Lanka, there were no designs made to withstand the tsunami waves. The levees were designed to protect against hurricanes, so we were interested in the level of floods, the amount of damage to the breach, the scour, and whether the walls were overtopped.

"We traveled with the geotechnical engineers and talked back and forth about what we observed. Because it's a flooding issue, I wasn't exactly sure how the geotechnical guys were going to weigh in. But there were some issues specifically relevant to their line of work. I was pleasantly surprised by that."

ASCE and the National Science Foundation will issue separate reports of their findings. ASCE's report will address both how and why the levees failed.

More information on these professional organizations can be found at these websites:

- *www.asce.org*
- *www.asce.org/instfound/techcomm_tclee.cfm*
- *www.copri.org*
- *www.ice.org*
- *www.geoinstitute.org*

## FROM STRANGERS TO A TEAM IN 48 HOURS

Imagine you're an operating room surgeon or nurse in the United States. You work with a hand-picked support staff using advanced equipment and technology. Then, imagine volunteering to join a team of medical personnel you've never met. For two weeks you travel to a part of the world where English is rarely spoken. You're part of a surgical team that operates on children and adults. You also might teach local medical staff.

Interplast is an organization that sends teams of medical personnel to perform free reconstructive plastic surgery for poor children and adults in developing countries. The teams typically number about a dozen people. Team members include plastic surgeons, anesthesiologists, pediatricians, operating and recovery room nurses, and team coordinators who also serve as translators.

Most often, Interplast teams perform surgeries to repair birth deformities, such as cleft lip and palate, that have a devastating lifetime impact if left untreated. Surgeries to perform burn reconstruction and repair hand injuries are also common. Team members also instruct local doctors in current techniques and conduct seminars on related medical topics.

Teams visit remote areas of developing countries. Recent destinations have included Peru, Vietnam, China, Ecuador, and Bangladesh. The intensity of the experience—up to 80 surgeries in a two-week trip—and the unfamiliar surroundings, language, and culture present steep challenges to the teams. Yet it usually takes only about 48 hours for the teams to bond.

Bill Schneider, MD, began as a volunteer plastic surgeon on an Interplast team. After five or so trips, he became a team leader. He served as a volunteer for over a decade before accepting the post of Interplast's chief medical officer. If anyone understands how these teams work, it's Schneider.

"We're plucking people from the finest health care systems and putting them in a strange place in a different culture to work for 10 to 12 hours a day." Once there, he says, they must function almost immediately as a team. No matter the circumstances, they are expected to perform at the same levels of quality and precision as in the United States.

"Team members often meet each other for the first time at the airport. They come together pretty fast. You're all there for the same purpose. You know you're going to work hard, and by the end of two weeks, you feel like you've known these people a much longer time." Though it might seem counterintuitive, Schneider says, the teams bond much faster when members don't know each other before the trip.

Interplast sends two or three first-time volunteers with experienced team members. Most volunteers go every year or every other year. Interplast works hard to send volunteers to new sites with new colleagues. "It works best for the team when everyone is on the same footing," Schneider says.

Schneider believes that because Interplast is a volunteer effort, the process is to some degree self-selecting. "People choose to do it and find us. I'm certain that's a big factor in why the teams work so well." Potential volunteers go through an extensive screening process that not only validates credentials but also looks for other success factors such as flexibility and being easy to work with.

Interplast's success in helping teams forge themselves into high performing units is due in no small part to meticulous preparation. Schneider and his colleagues leave little to chance. Six to eight weeks before departure, each team member receives a thick information packet. It covers everything from practical information about weather and current State Department briefs about the political climate, to what should be packed and the reports each member will write. First in the packet, though, is Interplast's code of conduct, containing guidelines on how members should act with each other and with their hosts, followed by specific rules for surgery, anesthesia, and nursing.

Then about a week before the trip, Schneider said, "We have a conference call with key senior staff and the entire team to go over all the issues. It works well to be very clear about the ground rules. The code of conduct is specific about our 'no sexual liaisons' policy and sexual harassment. We have found if liaisons develop, it is detrimental to the team, and it's just not acceptable."

The staff briefs the team leader in a separate telephone call. They stress the importance of daily team meetings, what to cover, how to get feedback, and a review of "what-if" scenarios. Team leaders are always only a phone call away from support in the United States, whether the issue is medical, personal, or political.

"We've seen everything from landing a team the day a civil war broke out to emergency procedures for a potential HIV contamination," Schneider says.

On location, the first order of business is a team meeting to review emergency scenarios. What happens if the power goes off, if the oxygen runs out, and a litany of other non-routine medical and surgical events.

Next, the team sets up a clinic to screen and schedule candidates for surgery. During this one-day event, the team might see as many as 150 people. A list of more than 30 bullet points guides the team in setting up and managing the clinic, right down to the sequence in which team members see potential patients.

"The clinic is the hardest part of the whole trip," Schneider says. "No physician in the U.S. screens 150 patients in a day." It has to be well organized.

A large hospital in a developing country might be a compound of twenty different buildings separated by large courtyards. Often, patients' families live in the courtyards. Many have traveled long distances together, hoping a family member can be treated.

"If you're doing surgery, you always want the next patient waiting, so you can move right along. In Vietnam, we were having trouble finding the patients because the complex was so large. And we were hard pressed to pronounce their names. So at our next team meeting, I put it out to the team," Schneider says. "It always amazed me how many good ideas you get from people who are involved. Within 10 minutes, we had created a solution, and from then on it flowed."

Establishing clearly designated roles avoids conflict and speeds up the process. "We're very clear that the anesthesiologist is in charge of the recovery room,

## 11  SOME SPECIAL TEAMS

and the pediatrician is in charge of patients on the floor. And there has to be a team leader, someone in charge over all," Schneider says.

"Heartrending decisions have to be made. You might be turning down a child and this may be their only chance. But rather than risk a surgery with a complicated outcome that might require follow-up with no ICU and no way of getting blood quickly, you have to say no. It's really hard. Everyone on the team wants to help the child. The team leader is the one who has to say we're not going to do this case."

It's critical that team members communicate well with each other, with local medical staff, and with the patients. Careful patient instruction is handled through fluent team members and local translators. Precise recordkeeping and documentation, not a small part of the venture, falls to the team coordinator. An extensive feedback reporting process for every team member enables Interplast to learn from each team to improve the next team's experience.

In her wrap-up trip report from Ecuador, one team member wrote, "This is the best team I have worked with to date! It jelled rapidly and functioned as a team immediately. Although there were several people who had never been on a[n Interplast] team before, they immediately knew what had to be done and how to do it. There was instant camaraderie."

More information on Interplast can be found at the website *www.interplast.org*.

# Additional Reading

Katzenbach, Jon R., and Douglas K. Smith. *The Wisdom of Teams: Creating the High-Performance Organization.* Harvard Business School Press.

Tharp, Twyla. *The Creative Habit: Learn It and Use It for Life.* Simon & Schuster.

Wheelan, Susan A. *Creating Effective Teams, A Guide for Members and Leaders.* SAGE Publications.

# Index

3M, 58, 62–63

## A

Academic expertise, 68
Agencies, government, 69
Allen, Paul, 1
American Society of Civil Engineering (ASCE), 78, 79, 80, 81, 82
Annual report, 75
Apy, Donald, 49
Assertiveness, 61
Audience, target, 46–47
Autonomy, 31, 32, 33

## B

Belonging on team, 43
Benefit of team, 1, 5, 7
Bennis, Warren, 45
Bowman, Adonna, 40
Bronson, Po, 46

## C

Capital, venture, 71
Client
    communication with, 48, 52–53
    thinking like, 60
Closing out project, 21, 75
Coasts, Oceans, Ports, and Rivers Institute (COPRI), 78, 80, 81, 83

Collaborative
    experiences, 5–6
    styles, 9–13
Commitment, 60–61
Communication, 32, 34, 45–55
    face-to-face, 46, 66
    flow, 48–49
    overload, 49
    repetition in, 52
    skills, 61
    unofficial, 53–54
    with client, 48, 52–53
    with management, 48
    with subteam, 47
    written, 48
Community, international, 69–70
Complexity in workplace, 1, 5
Conferences and symposia, 69
Conflict, 28, 37–44
    as dialogue, 39
    task vs. relationship, 38
Consultant, role of, 10
Contact network, 67
Contract group, 72
Creative working environment, 32, 34
Creativity, 55–58, 62
    exercise, 58
    indicators of, 56–57

steps to, 57–58

## D

Dalrymple, Tony, 83
Data General, 13
David-and-Goliath partnership, 71
Decision-making, 33, 42–43
Defining problem, 15–18
Definition of team, 3–4
Developers, as resource, 67–68
Developing solution, 20
Development, professional, 32, 34

## E

Earthquake Engineering Research Institute (EERI), 78
Edison, Thomas, 6
Edwards, Curt, 78–80
Einstein, Albert, 62
Emphasizing results, 75
Empowerment, 31–35
Empowerment Pyramid, 32–35
"Enormous Silly Problems," 51
Exercise, team creativity, 58
Experience, collaborative, 5–6
Expertise, academic, 68
External publicity, 74–75

## F

Finance group, internal, 71–72
Financial resources, 70–72
Ford, Henry, 1
Forming (Stage One), 25–26
Francis, Curt, 15, 16

## G

Gates, Bill, 1
Government agency, as resource, 69

## H

Headland, John, 80–83
Hewlett, Bill, 1
High-performance team, 29
Human talent, 66
Hurricane Katrina, 83

## I

Implementing solution, 21
Innovation, 1

Institute of Civil Engineers (ICE), 78, 81, 82
Internal finance group, 71–72
Internal marketing, 73
International community, 69–70
Interplast, 84–87
Intrapreneur, role of, 12

## J

Jordan, Michael, 40
Judgment, suspending, 61

## K

Kaboli, Parnian, 52
Katrina, Hurricane, 83
Kidder, Tracy, 13
Kirby, Connie, 40, 46

## L

Laurentine, Fredric, 35, 49, 60
Layout, office, 54
Legal group, as resource, 72
Lifecycle of project, 15–21
Listening, 45, 46
Lockheed Martin, 12–13

## M

Management, communication with, 48
Marketing, internal, 73
Motivation, 66

## N

Norming (Stage Three), 27, 31
Not belonging on team, 43

## O

Office layout, 54
Organizations, professional, 68–69
Overload, communication, 49
Ownership, 7, 31–36

## P

Packard, Dave, 1
Partnership, David-and-Goliath, 70
People, as resource, 66
Performance of team, 2, 3
Performing (Stage Four), 27–28, 31
Persistence, 62–63
Plan, project, 19
Poker chips, 40–41

# INDEX

Post-it notes, 62–63
Professional
    development, 32, 34
    organizations, 68–69
Project
    closing out, 21, 75
    lifecycle, 15–21
    plan, 19
    resources, 19, 33, 65–76
Publicity, 72–75
    external, 74–75
    internal, 73
Purchasing group, as resource, 72
Pyramid, Empowerment, 32–35

## R

Recognition and rewards, 32, 35
Recognizing stage of development, 28–29
Repetition in communication, 52
Report, annual, 75
Researchers, as resource, 67–68
Resource, 19, 32, 33, 65–75
    academic expertise as, 68
    conferences and symposia as, 69
    contact network as, 67
    contract group as, 72
    developers as, 67–68
    external publicity as, 74–75
    financial, 70–72
    government agency as, 69
    internal finance group as, 71–72
    internal marketing as, 73
    international community as, 69–70
    legal group as, 72
    partnership as, 70
    people as, 66
    professional organization as, 68–69
    publicity as, 72–73
    purchasing group as, 72
    researchers as, 67–68
    technology as, 66
    vendors as, 67–68
    venture capital as, 71
Results, emphasizing, 75
Rewards and recognition, 32, 35
Rodman, Dennis, 40
Roman, Harry T., 55, 71–72
Ross, Elliott, 59

## S

Satisfaction from team, 7
Schneider, Bill, 85–87
Selling
    ideas, 50–51
    solution, 20
Signs
    of poorly functioning team, 24
    of successful team, 4
    of well-functioning team, 23–24
Sirota, David, 31
Skills, communication, 61
Skunkworks, 12
Solution
    developing, 20
    implementing, 21
    selling, 20
*Soul of a New Machine, The*, 13
Sri Lanka, 80–83
Stages of team development, 25–28
    recognizing, 28–29
Steelcase, 53
Storming (Stage Two), 26–27
Subteam communication, 47
Successful team, signs of, 4
Support, 32, 33–34
Suspending judgment, 61
Symposia and conferences, 69

## T

Talent, human, 66
Target audience, 46–47
Team
    benefit of, 1, 5, 7
    creativity exercise, 58
    definition of, 3–4
    experience, 5
    high-performance, 29
    member, role of, 11
    performance, 2, 3
    poorly functioning, 24
    process, 42
    satisfaction from, 7
    signs of successful, 4
    stages of development, 25–28
    virtual, 49
    well-functioning, 23–24

Technical Council on Lifeline and
 Earthquake Engineering (TCLEE),
 78, 80, 81
Technology, as resource, 66
Thailand, 78–80
Thinking like client, 60
Thompson, Charles, 53
Trust, 32–33, 38
Tsunami, late 2004, 77–83
Tuckman, Bruce, 25
Tuckman model, 25

## U

Udall, Morris, 37
Unofficial communication, 53–54

## V

Vendors, as resource, 67–68
Venture capital, 71
Virtual teams, 49

## W

Wheelan, Susan, 3, 18, 23, 28, 39
Winshel, Steve, 17, 18, 49
Workplace complexity, 1, 5
Written communication, 48